The Snowboy

MARK BURNHOPE was born in 1982. He studied at London School of Theology before completing an MA in Creative Writing at Brunel University. His poems and reviews have appeared in a variety of print and online publications. He currently lives and writes in Bournemouth, with his partner, four stepchildren, two geckos and a greyhound. This is his first book of poetry.

The Snowboy

by
MARK BURNHOPE

LONDON

PUBLISHED BY SALT PUBLISHING
Acre House, 11–15 William Road, London NW1 3ER, United Kingdom

All rights reserved

© Mark Burnhope, 2011

The right of Mark Burnhope to be identified as the
author of this work has been asserted by him in accordance
with Section 77 of the Copyright, Designs and Patents Act 1988.

This book is in copyright. Subject to statutory exception
and to provisions of relevant collective licensing agreements,
no reproduction of any part may take place without the written
permission of Salt Publishing.

Salt Publishing 2011

Printed and bound in the United Kingdom by Lightning Source UK Ltd

Typeset in Swift 9.5 / 13

*This book is sold subject to the conditions that it shall not,
by way of trade or otherwise, be lent, re-sold, hired out,
or otherwise circulated without the publisher's prior consent
in any form of binding or cover other than that in which
it is published and without a similar condition including this
condition being imposed on the subsequent purchaser.*

ISBN 978 1 84471 873 3 pamphlet

1 3 5 7 9 8 6 4 2

*for Sarah and our family,
my five horizons*

Contents

Emoliage	1
The Little White Poem	2
To My Restored Example, Pinocchio	3
Wheelchair, Recast as a Site of Special Pastoral Interest	5
Milo Won't Go in the Water	6
The Ideal Bed	7
To My Familiar, Queequeg	9
To My Best-kept, Quasimodo	11
The Man Upstairs Drafts a Letter to the Councils	12
Our Jonah of Boscombe Pier	13
Twelve Steps towards Better Despair	14
Dream Invertebration	15
The Well and the Ceiling Rose	16
Queequeg (Reprise)	17
The Snowboy	18
Shinglehenge	19
Christogamy	20
The Centre	21
The Letting Tree	22
The Serpentine Verses	25
The House, the Church and Fisherman's Walk	26

Acknowledgements

I'm grateful to the editors of the publications in which some of these poems, or versions of them, first appeared: *Magma*, *Horizon Review*, *Nth Position*, *Ink Sweat & Tears* and *Other Lives*.

I'd also like to thank various poets for their friendship and critical input to poems in this book, including but not limited to: Ira Lightman, Andrew Philip, Angela Topping, Helen Ivory, AB Jackson, Tony Williams and Joshua Jones. Finally, massive thanks go to Chris and Jen Hamilton-Emery and Roddy Lumsden for their commitment and vision.

Lyrics from 'Carry Me' by The Levellers are reproduced by permission of On The Fiddle Publishing.

"For the listener, who listens in the snow"
— WALLACE STEVENS, The Snow Man . . .

Emoliage

The furor is on to find our blackest flower.
So far, we've only found the Prussian blue-
blood hues of the blootered finger
held to the board, and hammered.

The festival staff are sick and tired.

Black Pansy, never enough. Black Lily,
never enough. Black Iris, never enough.
Always an occasional vein to carry
a liniment-light to every extremity.

The festival staff are sick with worry.

The Little White Poem

White as an angel is the English child
— WILLIAM BLAKE, 'The Little Black Boy'

Goes to market.
Unfurls a great white sail
bright as the moonlight, pulled
taut behind the Kittiwake.

Drifts past and through the milk-
tipped waves of every era,
was used in various ways and al-
ways for honest purposes.

Goes aground. Opens to reveal
one thousand letters, none
of which were slaves,
only passengers.

Won't go far before
it eggs them on, up
to sweep chimneys,
polish our pipes.

Nothing if not
a white façade expression,
it learns by rote, or faces
the sweet crack of the cane.

To My Restored Example, Pinocchio

Real boy, I was wheeling by
my parish town's one toyshop
when I found you segment-slumped
in the window, and called you
Parochio, as in Paul returned to Saul.
I smiled, imagined you'd been healed
here on home ecclesiastical soil;
had left your strings lying
flaccid over an altar,
the cartilaginous ghost of all
you'd been before; had gone
and fucked this girl for the first
and last time, only to be caught
come morning by her father
and dropped off at the shop.
I relished these ideas: that no body
appeared to have had a hand
inside your restoration;
that even on that day you remained
my roughened, subdivided figurine
picked from the pine of good,
evil, and a little sick, truth
be told—part and brown parcel
of the hand-me-down furniture;
that when the vicar said: *I don't
know the number of hairs on your head.
However, I do know Gepetto, and have
for all your saw-dusted days. Would
you mind if I laid hands and prayed?*

no one in the pews
noticed your drawer-knob nose
aroused inside its socket as you said, *Nope.*

Wheelchair, Recast as a Site of Special Pastoral Interest

O evil scaffold, levelled
        and controlled by spirit.
O wing-black, spectral-silver mass;
crass imposition upon the meadow
formed of iron-carbon alloy—steel—
and foam; O folk dance of spoke,
        wheel, tyre, seat, the latter
        to which, flush out of the field,
        the executed calf
               and ewe contributed;
O cold construction site;
O social / medical model slag-
heap, and how for years
a man has worked on her,
        Bach in the background
               bounding over the vales.

Milo Won't Go in the Water

5 p.m. now and outside
soft light turns the Centre's
brick pinker than grey matter.

Inside, we meet Milo who
won't go in the water like
they've said he ought to.

See, they want to see him
raving and clowning,
and no, that's neither

here nor there
as morals go, just hydro-
therapy—bit demeaning

being flag-bearing hero,
chained tangoing bear
and buried treasure—

but make no bones: he will not
be the spacker who drowned
in the pool at anyone's Leisure.

The Ideal Bed

Double bed which shouldn't look
like this: so skewiff but no one on,
I can't even stand to smooth its sheet.
I try to circle round it, but my wheels
won't fit down the right side, the one
which, incidentally, I try to imagine hides
who we were five years ago: you standing
heaving the bed to and fro, trying to catch
our south-facing garden's light
(the bulbs were always blowing)
and me laughing; then afterwards
us, falling bed-long into this
self-same undividable iron maiden.
My nurse has just replaced our mattress
with a manmade, farcical memory-foam
thing: cures pressure sores faster.
You'd laugh if you could be here.
Remember shopping in IKEA,
wondering what kind of carpenter
constructed, folded, boxed and sold our bed?
*Hardly an artist, probably couldn't
have given an actual fuck*, you said.
When we got home the bed refused to stand
up in the room we'd meant for it. In its form,
we saw the ideal parts to shed:
a little off this surface, that corner.
We grew hungry, desperately so
pushed it against the larder door
so neither of us could hoard
when the waves crashed hard. Its back
was flimsy chipboard and would give

out in the year's most unnewsworthy
quake, if the front of the frame stayed.
So you sanded back for days, weeks,
months; pored over cookbooks,
catalogues and promotions; reclined
on the mattress like an ocean, faced
me and my canvas, and said, *Draw!*
(But the kitchen bulb was dying.)
Hardness the Lord made then tore:
the one you pushed aside to get past
the fact we never found
the perfect light to lie in.

To My Familiar, Queequeg

I too am tattooed.
I too tap away
nightly at an idol.

Show me a sailor who
hasn't savaged himself
and I will anchor a cyclone.

Our ink speaks
in *skin:* spins tales
of speared fins;

sirens found by fingering
tracks of sultry song
and then defiled.

The world turns
over like a novel
sex act requires

of a woman. I often
trail the geography
of the tethered body.

Once, I woke to find
your tentacles tightly
wrapped around me.

I wished to be tangled
safe, like Ishmael
finding in you his wife.

I wanted to compare
tattoos, remove tops
and trousers, and trace;

laugh at lines
blown out from excess
force by the hand, and time,

designs that lighten, slowly,
like flints in the sea.
For a while, Quee, we'd find

a world where the whale
is not white or dreadful. It's
a pale vessel, drifting, singing.

To My Best-kept, Quasimodo

*'When you're standing by the roadside
and it's a long way to go, I'll carry you'*
— THE LEVELLERS, 'Carry Me'

Like you, I have one eye
which is good, my other
a glossy, pussed growth,
a tumour. I would pluck it out,
say, I have sinned, Father—
seen far-and-away
the best of Esmeralda
through blue, stained-
glass panes: her sleight
of foot, bangled wrist,
Notre-Dame de Paris drowning
under her deft *Paparuda*.
But my better eye has seen us,
cliché cripple and Romani
gypsy, run to escape the flash-
storm of rain and paparazzi
curiosity forward-slash greed—
and so many spine-twisting stairs!—
to roost in my stone belfry:
feel the pull, hear the toll
whose light spell whispers
in the ear of a seed, makes
straight once-wasted bone.

The Man Upstairs Drafts a Letter to the Councils
obit anus, abit onus

Dear . . . no. My Loving . . . no. None of you
love me; neither should you, really. Look,
we never intended our peaceful landlady
to tumble those twenty steps to her death.

So I am about to pay forward the blame,
but do you blame me? Money's a root
of nearly every evil, don't you know. Hers
was a house but henceforth, let all places apply:

eatery, train tour, music venue, centre for
the frothing-over of mugs and mouths—
grant yourselves a great favour, raise
every lower surface to its higher. Fit a lift.

Our Jonah of Boscombe Pier
after Zbigniew Herbert

The Sperm whale had been beached
for so many days, signs were raised.
Caution: please keep off the rough,
barnacled blubber. Those are teeth
and not baleen for benign filtration.

But this enraptured tourist trod across

Leviathan's crash-mat spine, almost
plugged the blowhole with a boot
for he wished to re-enter into
those magisterial tales of whales
and the men who swallowed them.

Twelve Steps towards Better Despair

Rehearse its salt between your fingers often, vigorously.

Have it amalgamate into your petrol-slick tinted lethargy.

Write of the cormorant's yellow beak over her black body.

The iceberg: for a sound few seconds, it will stand
for solid material to marvel at. It need not sink your battleship
before you shy away from it. So don't bemoan its tip, thank it.

Make sure you have shouldered the world for a man who tried
dying—sorry, *died trying*—to climb a cliff summit,
or summat like it, to find a stronger sunlight.

Write of the good in global warming, icebergs melting, salt.

Recite names of the dead on your fingers often, vigorously.

Have their ashes sown into the stinking spumes of elegy.

Write of the widow's blonde wig over her black bodice.

Go fearlessly: for a modest seventy years we'll stand,
most of us men, to be gawped at; never forget that. So choose
your battles, and—if you buy—the best cruiser in the marina.

Make sure you have shouldered rope for a man who tied
skilfully: docked a boat and helped his lover onto the land
for both to stand under the cliffs and observe a cormorant.

Find and write of the good in swiftly dying—sorry, *flying*.

Dream Invertebration

The girl I'm seeing is given this dream.
You're always in it, she tells me, *but you're not
in the wheelchair.* I ask why. She replies:
It's undergoing correction in the workshop.

In the absence of a wheelchair, I am walking
on one paw like a cirque-du-freak performer.
My legs fuse to form a scorpion tail,
rainbow over my itchy, flaky scalp in a way

they couldn't of course, not even over a sofa.
I quiz her on further matters maybe less
conducive to this telling. Only, she's trying
to fiddle the door lock with a feather, I guess

in the fear that I might otherwise sting her.
I've been running her recurring dream through
a workshop on the 'net. No one gets it, telling me:
*Write where you'd have gone to if you had been in it.
You've a strong hand, go with it.* Ah, it stings.

The Well and the Ceiling Rose

the well sinks further
seemingly into the earth
when the moon is full

My brothers stole me from the house and hurled
me down the well. The moon was full and round
as hearts are full and round when pumping blood.

my mother's flush face
my father's burning-coal hearth
midnight dripping wax

There was no blood. It isn't cold, I told
my mother and my father when they found
me in the morning down the well. *I'm good*.

my brothers dried me beneath
the beams and the ceiling rose

Queequeg (Reprise)

Actually, Quee, before you go,
that tattoo I told you about,
a five-inch-wide labyrinth
etched in my left shoulder—
run your finger, or a Sharpie marker
round it; that's the path we travelled
remember, line we tugged, hauled
in every weather.

The Snowboy

No.   What to make
of what's becoming
nothing more than a mound of snow?

The one where he takes a thick grief
from its hook and wears it
        out to step into

                a freezer, and the glow
singes his eyes. For hours
the sky wavers over blues, to rest
back on transitory red
like blood a mother could not but have shed.

Which repeats
        on you; where

coals that lent him sight, a smile
and buttons have been removed
by the fingernail-wind, hands fanned, still
scraping blades against the barn.

    Where the one
we conceived on Christmas Eve
        pools, swaddles grass, clear as glass
        through which we might
        even have seen ourselves.

Shinglehenge

In order to recover
a kernel of our loss

let us build an altar
to someone smaller

less tangible, and none will
wonder why we raised her.

Christogamy

He sinks his support
in the sand: concrete pillar
to steel joist, blush taproot

to broadsword, thrusts it out, as a
punter to cross water
and any eye will tear to what it might.

∼

The doormat removes dirt
like a religious doctrine, and she
will not be one: *Thank God*

she tells him, leaving,
that you'll know
where to go when I'm gone.

∼

Every day after
the divorce, passersby lift
titbits and bobs

from their driveway skip:
a door, a windowpane,
a pistol-grip drill.

The Centre
for Graham

Christ is not your friend our lecturer said.
His evidence: ring-binder thin, but Lord,

we believed him. *I came not to bring peace,
but the sword. Not to unite, but to divide.*

∼

Boscombe Pier pierces

the sea. On either side of me
the promenade extends

arms that end
in bending wrists of cliff-side.

The land is dark, but look, his fists
pin-lit,

loosing breakers overnight.

The Letting Tree

'Excuse me. Are you the singing bush?'
'Follow the sea. Yea, ho, blow the man down.'
— The Three Amigos

*'To dwellers in a wood, almost every species of tree
has its voice as well as its feature.'*
— THOMAS HARDY

One tree holds its genealogy in
Sea Road, Boscombe. Roquette-dreaded,
stood outside the Urban Reef Café, it
was raised like a subject or the stakes,
was felled like flood defences.

It's overgrown.
Lend me your shears, it goes
to passing gardeners.

Frozen breeze crosses palm
and trunk; talks terracotta planter
into trembling, and the fronds
into letting free the legend
of Zacchaeus: took Jericho
Sycamore-fig branches
and turned to catch his call:

*Climb down. Let us
go to your home for breakfast.*

Back in the tax collector's house,
fresh bread baking in the range,
an age, or several ages, passed as Christ
led his eye along Zacchaeus' kitchen shelf:
ice, stone, bronze, iron
and all the eras golden.

They lit a fire, or lamp,
spread a Medieval table, dined
on skate and samphire, necked
so much Merlot, they lost track of time and so
washing the dishes finished in Enlightenment:

Zach, I'd say it's time
we raised the stakes, that subject
of money and productivity.
I'll appear in a pair and a spare, to place
some orders with your company.

The Internet Café in the Crescent
gets energy-drunk on tourists.
I can see Zacchaeus turning tables,
letting bone china crash
along with the first computer,
dashing into the back garden,
pining for that welcome-note
in a mute tree.

He tears back the outer bark,
falls into the phloem,
becomes cambium cell layer,
spins sapwood rings around his thumb,
dies in the heartwood's hold
so whenever I cross his palm and heckle:

Climb down. Let us break this
buckwheat loaf for breakfast, down
this wine before the bottle's thrown,

he has no defences, but
by the Boscombe high street light
asleep under the rafters
of our houses
he says to Christ,
I'm famished.

The Serpentine Verses

shuffle entirely free, immortal-
    coil through the chimney shaft
        breeze, blow briskly in
    by the redbrick's pores

hold your hood up high
    till your face, your fangs
        fill the whole hearth
    and man submits to man

his every rib still intact
    abdomen traced, and kissed
        for tonight, hallowed snake-seer
you need stomach no curses

let neither man
    believe his luck
        for here, as the leaves bend
    in the bedroom's holy book

bane of bane, and fashioned
    flash of flesh
    is about to fuck

The House, the Church and Fisherman's Walk

The non-discriminatory town accepts me,
sees no difference between a house
and hospital but for size, number of beds,
cadaver-count.
                  I dig my front casters
into the grass, of this derelict house
I wheel past daily.
Its windows, kaleidoscope-shattered,
twenty roof tiles missing, abused
by youth or age, bang on to me in Sign —
FOR SALE — what it says and has
for seemingly years.   The house
is seated at a church's right.
A beech bows over its fence,
weeps against that Beloved Body;
one day bites a thumb at the sad façade,
strokes its neck the next:
Ah! Dialogue, change,
at least to the state
of the church roof, the fence, the tree itself.
All that's skint and sorrowful watches.

Every Sunday, all the coastal churches
intercede for me, quick to unlock
the cells of my securely-guarded body.
Their petitions vary: 1) Evangelicals
in rhetoric-plate drive
the ghosts of Adam and Eve and all
their children (no longer one but Legion)
far from me; preach a future without a past
tense of *to suffer.* 2) Roman

Catholic doorframes carry my cross for me,
blood still fresh, wounds sashimi-raw.
They ask no more than that He,
Lemon Sole once slain,
look out for me, which is lovely
even if (slightly) lame.
                        The crux
of every prayer is much the same:
deliver me from the evil one,
whether he be damnation or just
a fortnight of light depression.

Pebbles, prayers, rosary beads
line the beds of Fisherman's Walk.
Flowers lay slain along the floor,
followers to the Toronto Blessing (1994).
Bins. Our foxes infiltrate to seek
and save and, let's be fair, to eat.

The lights on the street in the town on the coast
like me. Okay, some of their posts
are wonky but they shine on plaice
and pitta scraps thrown to swans
and us by prosperous families;
on them long-dead, gammy-legged
trembling out of the ground to dust
waders down, run to the ocean
where fishermen cast
without conditions or crutches.
All aboard the sprawling liquid ward
as Nurse Night flaps out a fitted sheet

they sleep on the tremulous sea; thusly
all their careful catches, care of a strain
of events too arcane to see, come to me.

www.ingramcontent.com/pod-product-compliance
Ingram Content Group UK Ltd.
Pitfield, Milton Keynes, MK11 3LW, UK
UKHW022203070425
457184UK00004B/32